The Burning Barn
A Chuck Polanski Novel

The Burning Barn
    A Chuck Polanski Novel

"The cruelest lie of all is the one they call love."

- Anonymous

ONE

It was another beautiful, sunny day when I first met Audrey Gibson.

I was sitting on the porch, sipping cold beer, soaking up the sun, and reading the daily newspaper when she walked into my life.

She had moved into Trish's old room several months before, but we'd never run into each other until that day. She was apparently a recluse, and although she wasn't necessarily unsociable, she wasn't the type to go in search of companionship, either.

I knew the feeling.

She had showed up on the front porch, carrying a book to read, a glass of lemonade, and a pack of Virginia Slims cigarettes. As she walked by me to take a seat in one of the empty lawn chairs, she smiled in greeting, I did the same, and she sat down next to me, the scent of her Chanel number five perfume waking my senses – in a good way, of course.

I had always been partial to the older perfumes, the classic scents. I had always worn Brut and Old Spice, and always would, too. Although I did consider myself pretty "hip" or cool for an older guy, my heart would always remain within the good old days of my own generation.

As she sat down, she took a deep breath, exhaled, leaned back in her chair, and closed her eyes, as if she was in a state of meditation.

Being the nosey old fart I'd always been, I cleared my throat and said, "Excuse me, Miss?"

Without opening her big blue eyes, she said, "Audrey Gibson. And you are?"

I said, "Chuck Polanski. Not to be nosey, but are you into yoga or something? Like meditation?"

Without opening her eyes once again, she smiled and said, "Something like that, yes."

Still not satisfied {and wanting to keep up a conversation with a very good looking lady} I said, "Something like that? That's not very specific."

She opened her eyes, then, and although the ocean blue color stood out like sore thumb, I could see beyond the color of her eyes, and almost into her soul.

The *pain* in her soul. Her big blue eyes betrayed what really lay beneath it all. Just like Patty's eyes had last year – before she took her own life.

She said, "I was thinking about my daughter, Sherri. She would have been forty-five years old today."

"Would have been?" I said, and suddenly wished I hadn't, not wanting to pry too much into her private life.

She said, "Yes. She died many years ago, nineteen-seventy-five, to be exact."

I said, "I'm so sorry for your loss, we don't have to talk about it if you don't want to."

She turned to me and said, "It's fine, Mr Polanski, I don't mind talking about it. It helps to keep her memory alive. That's why I like to sit out here, in the sunshine, and close my eyes and day dream of long ago, when my daughter and I would do things together, like talk walks or go to the beach. It helps me cope."

I said, "Yes, I can understand that all too well."

She said, "I doubt that, Mr Polanski."

Taken back by her remark at first, I said, "Meaning?"

She said, "My daughter was *murdered*, Mr Polanksi. Can you honestly say you can understand that concept?"

Feeling like a fool at that moment, I said, "No, I guess I can't. Sorry."

She said, "It's fine, Mr Polanski, you had no way of knowing."

There were a few moments of uncomfortable silence, then she said, "So, I hear you are a writer."

I said, "*Aspiring* writer, yes."

She lit one of her cigarettes, and said, "I also understand that you helped to solve a local crime last year. Is that true?"

I said, "Yes, I did, but it was just by blind luck, actually."

She said, "Blind luck is better than no luck, is it not?"

Thinking it over, I said, "Yes, I guess you're right."

She looked me straight in the eyes then, and said, "Mr Polanski, may I ask you a favor? It's a *big* favor, so I will completely understand if you choose not to do so."

I sipped my beer and said, "You won't ever know unless you ask. I'm listening."

She said, "Would you consider looking into my daughter's case? Her killer was never apprehended."

I didn't know what to say at first. I had street smarts, yes, and was good at doing research, but other than my dogged sense of determination, I was no real sleuth, amateur or otherwise.

I said, "Well, I could, yes, but I most definitely can't *promise* you anything."

She smiled and said, "Fair enough. But keep in mind, I can't afford to pay you much for your services."

Waving the remark off, I said, "Since I'm not a *real* detective, my services are free of charge. Fair enough?"

She said, "More than fair. But I feel like I should repay you somehow."

Mulling it over, I said, "How about dinner tonight? I bet you are a good cook."

She said, jokingly, "Why, Mr Polanski, are you asking me out on a date?"

I smiled and said, "I guess I am, but, it will be all business before pleasure. Fair enough?"

Standing to leave, she said, "Fair enough. Shall we say seven o'clock, here on the front porch? We'll have ourselves a little sunset picnic."

Out of respect, I stood up, and said, "It's a date. I'll bring the wine."

She smiled, nodded her head in understanding, and walked inside without another word.

I just sat there for several minutes, excited about our dinner date, but also feeling a little nervous at the same time.

Then I went inside, took a shower, and poured myself a glass of single malt.

TWO

She showed up right on time, carrying a small wicker basket containing our dinner.

She had prepared a simple but tasty dinner; salami and swiss on rye bread with mayo. I brought a simple red wine, and it seemed to enhance the flavor of the lunchmeat.

So far, so good.

As we sat in our lawn chairs, nibbling on our sandwiches and sipping wine, she suddenly and unexpectedly brought up the subject of her daughter's murder case, which I had thought she would have saved until after our meal.

She said, "So, Mr Polanski, I understand you are definitely a determined man when it comes to your research."

I said, "I can be, yes. May I ask where you have heard about me?"

She cracked a sly little grin, and said, "I wouldn't have approached you today without looking into your background first, Mr Polanski."

Sipping my wine, I said, "Damn. And I thought it was my good looks and winning personality."

She giggled and said, "Well, and that too, of course."

I said, "So, yes, I am a very determined man when I am working a case. But bear in mind, I am not only just a true crime buff, but I tend to drink a lot from time to time too. I look upon it as a coping mechanism."

She said, "I think we all have our own way of coping with unpleasant situations, Mr Polanski, as long as it doesn't effect your performance."

I said, "You just let me worry about that, Miss Gibson."

She said, "Very well. Now, what are your plans for the research?"

I said, "Well, I usually begin by logging into the internet, and seeing what I can find there first. These days, there is a ton of info we don't even know about on murder cases, digital files, etc."

She said, "I have a file folder upstairs, I have been collecting my own files for years now, if that would help."

I said, "Oh yes, I'd love to look at the file."

She sipped her wine and said, "Okie dokie, then. I will go grab it after dinner, and let you look it over."

So, finished our dinner, and afterward, she went upstairs and retrieved the old files. Then she excused herself for the evening, and went back to her room.

I sat on the couch, looking over her file folder, and sipping single malt. Before I knew it, it was past midnight, and I had fallen asleep.

THREE

I didn't wake up until the next morning, when Audrey knocked on my door.

Scrambling to look presentable, I didn't answer the door until the third knock. As I opened the door, in all of my hungover, disheveled glory, there she was, as fresh and pretty as the morning dew. Needless to say, I wanted to disappear.

She said, "Well, Mr Polanksi. Have I interrupted something?"

I could feel my face flush with embarrassment as I said, "No ma'am. I haven't been awake very long."

She said, "That's obvious. Should I come back later, after you're had a chance to gather yourself?"

I said, "Yes, if you wouldn't mind."

Cracking that cute little sly grin again, she said, "Fine, then. Say about an hour?"

I said, "Yes, ma'am, if you don't mind."

She said, "Fine then. And please, stop calling me ma'am. It makes me feel old. Just call me Audrey."

I said, "Fine then. And you can call me Chuck."

"Workds for me," she said, and turned to walk back upstairs. As she walked up the old rickety staircase, I couldn't help but notice she could brighten up even the gloomiest of places.

#

An hour later, like clockwork, there was another knock at my door.

Clean and shaven and wearing my trusty Old Spice cologne, I opened the door to see that she, too, had spruced up a bit – but not that she needed to do so for my sake.

She said, "Well, Chuck. You look like a totally different man."

I grinned and said, "Is that good or bad?"

She grinned back and said, "Maybe a little of both?"

Stepping aside to let her in, I said, "Fair enough."

#

As we both took a seat at the kitchen table, she glanced around the room and said, "Not bad for your typical bachelor pad."

I grinned and said, "Is that good or bad?"

She stifled a giggle and said, "Good, considering your "average" bachelor can tend to be a tad bit unorganized."

"Messy, in other words?" I said, lighting a cigarette.

She said, "That's phrasing it politely, but yes, the word messy would work."

I said, jokingly, "I'm so glad I meet with your approval so far, my dear."

There was that cute little sly grin again, as she lit a cigarette and said, "So, Chuck. Have you looked at the file folder yet?"

I said, "Yes, last night. I must say, you have

assembled quite the history on the case."

She said, "When it is left up to *yourself* to solve it, you must be as meticulous as possible."

"Oh, I agree," I said, and could feel my guts churning, my body jonesing for the demon alcohol. "Would you if I indulged in a glass of wine? It might help me wake up a bit."

She said, "You know, that does sound good. Would you pour me a glass as well?"

"Sure," I said, and retrieved the wine bottle and two glasses from the kitchen counter. I sat back down, poured our wine, and said, "Now, that's better."

Sipping her wine, she said, "Yes, it is. Now, as you were saying about the file folder?"

Sipping my wine, I said, "There is a lot of useful info in there, yes, but I still want to scour the internet for some more."

She said, "Please, be my guest."

I said, "Now, bear in mind, this *is* a thirty year old case, so don't expect any miracles here. Sorry, just trying to be honest."

She said, "I wouldn't want it any other way, Chuck. And yes, I am used to disappointment as far as this case is concerned, so please don't feel guilty if your investigation doesn't pan out."

I said, "Thank you. Now, it said in your file folder, that there was witness to this crime?"

She said, "Yes, her boyfriend, Larry Alton. But he was a witness to the abduction, not the crime itself."

I said, "Yes, of course. Sorry."

Blinking away tears, she said, "They locked him in the trunk of his car, and left him to smother to death."

I said, "They? There was more than one

abductor?"

She said, "Yes. Larry said it was a man and a woman, both of them dirty and unkept, and reeked of alcohol and marijuana."

I said, "They could have been transients then, just passing through."

She shook her head and said, "I don't think so. Over the next few years, there even more crimes of the same type, and same descriptions."

I then asked the question I'd been dreading to ask, but thought I needed to know. I said, "And your daughter?"

Wiping away tears with a napkin, she cleared her throat and said, "She was taken to an old horse barn nearby, where they proceeded to beat her, rape her, and then stabbed her to death. One of the detectives on the scene told the media that the scene was so bloody, it made the Charles Manson murders seem *mild* in comparison."

I felt my stomach almost lurch as I said, "Oh my God, I'm so sorry Audrey."

She said, "Then they set the barn on fire, in order to destroy any evidence, no doubt. I had to give my daughter a closed casket funeral service."

I said, "I don't know how you even made it through all of this."

Lighting another cigarette, she said, "I knew I *had* to make it through, for my daughter's sake."

I said, "You are a very strong woman, Audrey, and I am very proud to have made your acquaintance."

She forced a smile and said, "Thank you, Chuck, and the feeling is mutual."

I said, "I appreciate that, but I'm nobody special,

believe me."

She said, "You are to me. You are taking my case on for *free*, and seem *sincere* in wanting to help me. That is more than anyone else has ever done for me."

I said, "Thank you, Audrey. That means a lot coming from you."

She said, "You're very welcome. Now, Chuck, why don't we stop talking about depressing subjects for now, and have a glass of wine on the front porch? It's another beautiful day out there."

My guts still jonesing for more of the demon alcohol, I said, "I think that sounds like a wonderful idea."

FOUR

It really was a beautiful day.

As we sat on the porch, soaking up the sun, sipping wine, and exchanging cheerful banter, it seemed as though the day would never end, and we would someday look back on that day fondly, keeping it locked away in our memory palace forever.

That is, until Audrey suddenly broke down sobbing, her tears flowing like rain.

Then there was the *wailing*.

I don't know if you've ever heard a woman who has lost child – and in such a terrible way – wailing before, but it is a sound like no other.

It is a sound that comes deep from within a heart and soul that's been forever torn asunder, that will never really heal. I will never forget that sound, either.

Then, a few moments later, just as quickly as it had all begun, she stopped, just rocking back and forth in her lawn chair, with her face in her hands. I stood up, knelt down next to her, and, taking one of her trembling hands in my own, and said, "It's alright, Audrey. I'll be here for you."

She raised her head, forcing a smile, and said, "I know that, and thank you."

I said, "Are you going to be alright? We can cancel this day's festivities if you're not up to it."

She said, "No, I'll be fine. Sometimes, you just

have to let it all out, you know?"

Oh yes, I knew all too well. The day my Missy cat died, I know I too wailed with heartache, although I doubt it was anything like Audrey's wailing.

I said, "Been there, done that. But unlike myself, you have someone to see you through it all."

She squeezed my hand gently, and said, "Yes, I do. Speaking of which, why don't you open another bottle of wine, and let's enjoy the rest of the day."

I said, "I'm sorry, but I don't have any wine left. I'm normally a single malt man myself, and the occasional beer."

She said, "I like a cold beer now and then."

Standing to my feet, I said, "Coming right up!"

#

A few minutes later, as I sipped single malt and Audrey sipped cold beer, she had regaled me with stories from her past; her teenage years, her marriage to Sherri's father and his subsequent and untimely death, as well as her long road, alone, to find her daughter's killer.

By the time she was finished, I felt as though I'd known her forever. She just had that *way* about her.

A way that was slowly but surely stealing my heart, but I wasn't going to tell her about my feelings, she had enough on her mind already.

As she sat sipping her beer and watching the sun slowly fading beyond the horizon – me sharing *my* sunset with her – she said, "Did I tell you about that happened to Larry? Sherri's boyfriend?"

I said, "No, not yet."

She said, "His story was a sad one, too. After all

that happened to him – including Sherri's death – he ended up the object of suspicion and ridicule, instead of one of sympathy or compassion."

"How so?" I said, sipping my drink.

She lit a cigarette and said, "He had spent all that time reliving the trauma and being burdened with vicious rumors and small town gossip. Then, in nineteen-ninety-eight, he died in a mysterious *fire*."

I said, "Just like the burning barn."

She said, "Yes, exactly."

I said, "Suicide, you think?"

She said, "Maybe, but I doubt it. Yet another mystery that has remained unsolved all these years."

I said, "Hopefully not for much longer."

Forcing another smile, she said, "Thank you."

I said, "I noticed in your file folder, there was a man who was questioned about the murder, but he was eventually cleared of any suspicion."

She said, "Ah, yes. Mr Wade Mulley. He was an interesting character, he was, but apparently not guilty of anything other than being an oddball."

I said, "Are you sure about that? In your file folder, it says that he was questioned in several other cases, including a rape case."

"Yes," she said, sipping her beer. "But, he was also cleared of those cases, too."

I said, "Well, I still think he's worth looking into, that is, if he's still alive."

She said, "Oh, he is still around. I see him cruising through town now and then, driving an old beat up station wagon."

I said, "Would you mind if I took a good look at him first, just to satisfy my own morbid curiosity?"

She grinned and said, "Sure, why not? I mean, you are the sleuth here, not me."

I said, "Thank you. I'll get right on it tomorrow morning."

She cracked that cute little sly grin of hers, and said, "And until then?"

I said, "Until then? Let's just sit here and watch the sunset, and relax."

She scooted her lawn chair closer to my own, grasped my right hand gently in her own, and said, "I think that's a wonderful idea."

As we sat there, hand in hand, watching the sunset, I was reminded of an old saying I'd heard as teenger.

Of all the cruel lies they tell you, the cruelest one is the one they call love.

I sipped my drink, closed my eyes, and tried to block that thought from my mind.

I think she did, too.

FIVE

Sherri opened her eyes to find herself in a old, weather-beaten barn-house. Her hands were tied behind her back and she was gagged. She shook slightly as a breeze came through the broken window. She looked down and saw that the person that had kidnapped her had removed her clothes, leaving her in her bra and underwear. As she looked up again, she saw her kidnapper coming back in from outside. His name was Wade.

She knew his name because she'd heard it mentioned numerous times on the way to the barn, while she was lying in the back seat of a stranger's car. She'd heard a woman's voice too, but no name was mentioned.

What her captors had done with her boyfriend, Larry, she did not know. But judging by her current situation, it might be better for her current frame of mind if she didn't know.

The man named Wade was holding a bottle of cheap liquor. His eyes were bloodshot and wild and his face pale. He looked more like a ghost than a man.

She felt another shiver as he spoke to her in a deep, guttural tone of voice. "Are we comfy? I hope so, because we are going to have some fun."

Whatever type of 'fun' he was speaking of she could just imagine, but she tried her best to block it from her mind. Not that it would do her any good in the end.

"Where is my boyfriend?" she asked, thinking more of his welfare than her own. She'd decided she did want to know, no matter how hard it might be to hear about his fate.

Wade just grinned and said, "No need to worry about him, babe. He's going to be just fine." He lit a cigarette and exhaled. "You should be more concerned with what I'm getting ready to do to you."

Knowing now that her fate was sealed as soon as she woke up in the barn, she lost interest quickly in trying to pacify this creep. She said, "Over my dead body, you will."

He stepped closer, grinning again. He reached behind him and pulled a long, sharp knife from his belt. He said, "Well, that can be arranged.."

Were those what the last few moments of Sherri Gibson's life were *really* like? As a writer of non-fiction, I'd say my theory, once again, was most likely mild in comparison.

The horrific crimes had authorities and local residents alike dumbfounded as well as terrified for years, due to the brutal and vicious nature of the crimes.

And, in the thick of it all, Audrey, helpless and left behind to pick up the pieces of her life as best she could.

But I was here now, and I intended to find Mr Mulley, follow him, and eventually come up with something that would hang him for the crime.

That is, *if* he was guilty.

I was no real detective, mind you, but my street smarts were telling me I was on the right trail.

Just like the little voices in my head used to tell

me things, now my street smarts were doing the same.

And...if he was guilty, who was his female cohort in crime? A girlfriend? His wife?

I intended to find out.

Now, with Audrey upstairs and asleep on her couch, self medicated and getting some much needed slumber, it was time for Chuck Polanksi, full time drunk and part time sleuth, to get to work.

#

As I sat there glancing over her file folder again, I could see that Wade's last known address was right outside of town, right past Pearl City, one of the rural route numbers, so I decided to wait until after dark, and take a casual stroll down the road to see if he still lived there.

But before I could leave, Miss Audrey woke up.

#

I was sititng at the kitchen table, sipping some single malt and planning my strategy, when there was a light tapping at my door.

Knowing who it was by the tapping, a big grin spread across my face as I went to answer the door. She had a way of making me grin like a lovestruck school boy, and I will never forget that, either.

I opened the door to see her dressed in a pair of fuzzy house slippers, a long floral night robe, and her hair tied back in a bun. She looked like someone's grandmother, like you'd see in a Norman Rockwell painting – except a lot better.

She said, "Well, good evening Chuck."

I said, "Good evening, Miss Audrey. I trust you got some well deserved sleep?"

Yawning, she said, "Oh yes, I feel much better now. By the way, next time we sit on the porch to watch the sunset? Please, limit me on my beer consumption."

I grinned and said, "So, we have a slight hangover, do we?"

She said, "I could use some coffee."

I said, "It's the instant stuff. Is that okay?"

She said, "Just as long as it's coffee."

I said, "Well, come in and have a seat at the table, then."

As she sat down and lit a cigarette, I made the coffee, placed it down on the table in front of her, and said, "Sorry, I don't have any cream or sugar."

She said, "It's fine, I like my coffee black."

I sat down, lit a cigarette and sipped my single malt. She said, "So, I see you haven't quite reached your quota for the day yet."

I said, "Sorry."

She said, "It's none of my business, just an observation."

I said, "Fair enough. But no, I haven't quite met my quota just yet. To be honest, it keeps me on an even keel, and at times, even helps me concentrate."

She raised her coffee cup in a mock toast, and said, "Whatever works for you. Speaking of which, how are your plans coming along?"

I said, "Not too bad. I'm planning to take a walk down rural route three this evening, to see if Mr Mulley still resides there."

She said, "And if he doesn't?"

I said, "Then I'll come up with another plan. I'm pretty street smart, you know?"

"She cracked that sly grin of hers again, and said, "Oh, I'm quite sure of that."

I said, "Thank you for the vote of confidence."

She said, "Am I bothering you? I can drop by tomorrow if I am."

I said, "Oh no, not at all. I appreciate the company, actually." *Her company, that is.*

She said, "So, you're not a totally confirmed bachelor after all?"

I said, "Okay, you caught me in a lie."

She grinned and said, "Let's just call it a little white lie, shall we?"

"Deal," I said, and sipped my drink.

She yawned again, sipped her coffee, and said, "Well, not to be unsociable, but I think I need some more sleep."

I said, "That's understandable. I'll just fill you in tomorrow morning on what happens tonight."

Standing to leave, she said, "Sounds like a good plan to me."

As she walked toward the door, I couldn't hold back any longer, and I said, "By the way, you look very pretty tonight."

Her face flushed with embarrassment, she turned to me and said, "And you, Mr Polanski, have been a bachelor too long."

Then was she was gone.

She was right about what she said, too.

I'd been alone way too long.

SIX

After she left, I had prepared my travel bag.

The usual stuff; a small flashlight, a pack of cigarettes, a half pint for the road. I know it doesn't sound too professional, but it doesn't take much to just snoop around someone's home after dark.

That, and a set of balls.

Which, luckily for me, I had in abundance.

#

I set out around midnight.

By then, most folks in my quaint little town were either asleep, or running the streets looking for something to do. I wasn't too concerned with the latter; I would fit right in without too much suspicion.

As I passed by the entrance to Pearl City, and onward toward route three, I could already see the lights of the houses in the distance. If the info I found on the internet was correct, Wade's tiny little ramshackle house, left to him by his parents, would be the third house on the right.

As I slowly approached the homes, keeping within the shadows as much as I could, I stopped, lit a cigarette, took a sip from the half pint, and took a breather before moving on.

As I moved forward again, I could see that Wade's

old house looked possibly abandoned.

Several of the windows were boarded up, and the weeds in the yard were knee high. No lights.

No sign of life.

As I stepped forward again, training my little flashlight on the back of the property, the sound of a gun being cocked stopped me dead in my tracks.

Then, a voice. Deep and raspy, with a purposeful tone to it. "And just who in the hell are you, anyway, sneaking around in my back yard?"

I slowly turned around, with my hands raised high in the air, to see a tall, lanky fella dressed in overalls and a t-shirt, holding a shotgun. I said, "Sorry, mister. I was just looking for the old Wade house."

Lowering the shotgun just a tad bit, the fella said, "Oh hell, boy. That place has been empty for years now. Wade lived there for a while after his folks died, but I ain't seen him in a long time, neither."

I said, "Well, I guess I wasted my time, then. You have a good night, and sorry about trespassing."

As I turned to leave, the fella said, "No harm done, I guess. By the way, why are you looking for Wade, anyway?"

I said, "Oh, he's just an old friend, that's all. I just stopped by to say hi."

The old fella said, "Well, if you are an old buddy of Wade's, I don't want your worthless ass hanging around my place, anyway."

I didn't bother replying to his remark as I quickly darted back into the shadows, feeling very lucky not to have my ass filled with buckshot.

SEVEN

I arrived back at my place around two-thirty am.

As I walked up to the front porch, there was Audrey, in her night robe and slippers, sitting in one of the lawn chairs, smoking a cigarette and sipping coffee.

As I climbed the front porch steps, she said, "I couldn't sleep."

Sitting down on the top step, I said, "I can see that."

She said, "In all honesty, I couldn't sleep thinking about you, all alone out there in the dark."

I said, "That's very sweet of you, but I can handle myself."

She grinned and said, "Of that I have no doubt."

I took a drink from the half pint and said, "Well, the trip to Wade's old place was a bust. The house was apparently abandoned years ago."

She said, "I should have figured as much. So, now what, my favorite amateur sleuth?"

"Plan B." I said.

She said, "Which is?"

I said, "Which is, I pay a visit to some of his old stomping grounds. You know, taverns and the like."

She said, "Doesn't that sound a tad bit dangerous? I mean, I would imagine he didn't keep the best of company."

I said, "No more dangerous than having some

hillbilly asshole pointing a shotgun at me in the dark."

She said, "Come again?"

Sipping the half pint, I said, "Some old redneck with a shotgun let me know he didn't appreciate me lurking around too close to his property, that's all. I'm fine."

She said, "I'm sorry, Chuck."

I said, "No reason to be. It comes with the territory."

She sat up and said, "Well, any time you feel too pressured by it all, I'll understand."

I said, "Thank you my dear. Now, why don't we both get a good night's sleep, and meet back here in the morning?"

Standing to her feet, she said, "That sounds like a great idea. Say, around nine am?"

"It's a date," I said, and we both walked inside, as she reached out and grasped my hand gently in her own. She looked me directly in the eyes and said, "Please, don't take this the wrong way."

Then she leaned in and kissed me.

On the lips.

It wasn't just a friendly kiss, either. It was a passionate kiss.

The kind of kiss shared by two lovers.

When it was over, she cracked that sly grin again and said, "I just *had* to know, that's all."

Feeling my heart beating a thousand miles an hour in my chest, I said, "And?"

She said, "I'll think about it, and let you know."

With that, she was gone, up the stairs and out of sight.

I just stood there for a few moments, catching my

breath, and walked into my apartment, closing the door behind me just in time to break down crying.

But, they were happy tears.

EIGHT

The next morning around nine am, we were already sitting on the porch, sipping some spiked coffee and exchanging cheerful banter as usual.

But our pleasant conversation soon turned to the kiss we'd shared the night before, which I was sure it would, at least on my part, anyway.

Sipping my coffee, allowing the single malt work it's magic on my tongue, I said, "So, not to put you on the spot, but, what was that kiss all about last night?"

Sipping her coffee, she said, "Like I said, I just needed to know, that's all."

I said, "I know that, but *what* was it you needed to know?"

She took another sip of her coffee, took a deep breath, and started to speak, until a familiar car pulled up out front, grabbing my attention.

The old dark blue Sedan.

Harley Crow's Sedan.

I said, "Oh shit, not now."

Audrey said, "What's wrong?"

I said, "I'll fill you in later."

By that time, Harley was already approaching the front porch, stopping to light a cigarette. After exhaling, he said, "Well, if it isn't the famous writer. What are you working on lately, if I may ask?"

I said, jokingly, "Well, if it isn't Deputy Barney

Fife. Have you and Sheriff Andy been chasing down any bad guys lately?"

Crow said, "Real funny."

I said, sarcastically, "I try."

He said, "Well, you would have to be better at comedy than you are at taking friendly advice."

I said, "Meaning?"

He said, "Don't play stupid. You damn well know what I'm talking about, Polanski."

I said, "No, I don't, actually. Enlighten me."

He sat down on the steps and said, "I heard you've been snooping around rural route three after dark now, making folks feel uneasy."

Audrey broke into the conversation then, saying, "Excuse me, Mister?"

Crow said, politely, "Harley Crow, ma'am. I'm a Detective."

She said, "Well, Mr Crow, the only reason he was down there was he was doing me a favor."

Crow said, "With all due respect, ma'am, your favor almost got his head blown off."

She said, "I heard. But it didn't happen that way. So, why don't you mind your own business?"

Crow said, "I'm sorry, ma'am, but I can't do that."

She said, "And stop calling me ma'am. I'm not ancient just yet."

Crow said, "Of course, I apologize." Then he turned to me and said, "I heard you were down there looking for Wade Mulley."

I said, "Yes I was. But he has apparently flown the coop."

Crow said, "Want some more good advice?"

I said, "Not really, but I'm sure you will give it to

me regardless. I'm listening."

Crow said, "You best stay away from him, even if you do find him. That whole family is batshit crazy."

I said, "I've already gathered that, but I've also already made a promise."

Crow said, "A promise to get your head blown off? That's a whole different kind of stupid."

Audrey broke in again and said, "Helping to lock up a vicious killer isn't stupid, Mr Crow, it's justice."

Crow said, "Meaning?"

I broke into the conversation and said, "I'm just researching for a new book, that's all. No harm done."

Standing to leave, Crow said, "Well, best keep it that way, Polanski."

We watched as he walked back to his Sedan and opened the driver's side door, then I said, "Oh, and Mr Crow?"

Crow said, "Yeah, yeah, I know. I can go screw myself."

With that, he was gone, no doubt on his way to harrassing someone else. Glaring at him as he pulled away, Audrey said, "I don't like him."

I said, "Oh, he's not that bad. He just thinks that he has to be a real prick to get his point across."

She said, "I still don't like him."

Sipping my coffee, I said, "Good, me neither."

Cracking that cute little sly grin of hers, she said, "Now, where were we before we were so rudely interrupted?"

I said, "Ah, yes. That sweet little smooch you gave me last night."

She said, "I just wanted to know how it felt to feel alive again."

I said, "And?"

She said, "I'm beginning to feel alive again for the first time in years."

I said, "Well, glad I could help."

Flashing me a playful wink, she said, "Although, next time, you could kiss me back."

Feeling sort of awkward but excited at the same time, I said, "Deal."

She said, "Now, let's get to work on the case."

I said, "I was afraid you were going to say that."

NINE

We sat there for a while, basking in the morning sun and both of us feeling alive again.

I felt more alive in her company than I had in my entire life, actually, and was secretly praying it would never end.

That's when my newest rescue kitty, Patty, showed up on the porch, looking like she'd been rode hard and hung up wet.

I said, "Well, there you are, you little tramp."

She rubbed her tail against my legs as Audrey said, "You didn't tell me you had a kitty."

I said, "I do, I guess. She takes off sometimes for two or three days, but always comes back home. I am beginning to think she is very promiscuous."

Having to stifle a laugh, she said, "Well, it's a *cat*, my dear. Just like all other living beings, she has instincts, and needs."

I said, "Yeah, well, I can't afford to feed a whole apartment full of baby tramps, either."

She said, "I get it. But she is awful sweet and precious, you know."

She was right about that. As I leaned down to pick Patty up, she was already purring up a storm and trying to lick my face. She had a look in her eyes like she was thinking, *Yeah, I'm a naughty girl sometimes, but you still LOVE me, don't you, you old fart?*

I hugged her, listening to her tiny little heart beating, and I found myself wondering what it would be like laying next to Audrey, listening to her heart beating in sinc with my own.

I said to Audrey, "Well, why don't we take this little munchkin inside, clean her up, and give her something to eat?"

She said, "Sounds like a plan. Then what shall we do?"

I said, "Discuss the case, of course."

She said, "Of course."

But she didn't seem too sure this time.

#

A short time later, as we sat at the table watching Patty scarf up some tuna patte, and discussing the case, she had seemed to have lost interest, at least temporarily.

Confused by her apparent lack of interest, I said, "Penny for your thoughts?"

Sipping some more fortified coffee, she said, "I've been thinking"

I said, "Care to enlighten me?"

She said, "About my daughter, I mean. Do you think she would *really* want me to carry on like this, year after year, decade after decade, and come up with nothing but more heartache?"

I said, "I didn't know your daughter, of course, but, by what you've told me about her, I don't think she would want you to keep on suffering, no, but at the same time, she wouoldn't want you to give up so easily, on something that was so important to you, either."

Audrey said, "You may be right about the latter,

but, I'm slowly but surely growing very tired as well as very disillusioned about it all, too."

I reached across the table, grasped her right hand gently in my own, and said, "Ill be here for you, no matter what you decide, remember?"

Forcing a smile, she said, "Yes, I remember, my dear, and thank you so much for your patience and understanding."

I said, "You're very welcome. Now, shall we discuss my so called "plan B," or would you rather do this on another day?"

She forced a smile again, and said, "You keep on spiking my coffee, and I'm sure I can get through it all."

So I did.

Spiked my own coffee, too.

An hour later, I had come up with plan B.

TEN

My plan B was as follows.

I would wait until around dusk again, when the local bar patrons would be getting off work and ready to suck down cold beer until their eyeballs popped out, and then insert myself into the crowd, and listen to their loose tongues wagging, their inhibitions all but lost, jabbering on about things they would normally keep a secret.

And, of course, I would be listening to it all, as best I could, and inserting myself into some of these conversations, and drop an unobvious hint here and there, about Wade Mulley, who was just an old friend.

As I sat at the kitchen table, finishing off a good sandwich Audrey had made for me, and chasing it down with cold beer, I heard my front door creak open, and there she was, in all of her glory, standing there dressed in long, floral sundress, open toed sandals, and her hair tied back, with a small sunflower placed behind one ear.

Dumb struck by her natural beauty, almost speechless at first, I said, "Wow."

She said, jokingly, "Is that all you have to say? *Wow?* How old are you? Fifteen?"

I stood up and said, "If I told you what I was *really* thinking, you would most likely think I was a very naughty boy."

Cracking that trademark, sly grin again, she said,

"Down, boy. Be a good boy. There's plenty of time for romance later."

I said, "Is that an offer?"

She lit a cigarette and said, "We'll see."

I said, "Don't play games with my heart, woman."

She said, "Chuck, be honest with me. *Why* is it, you find me so desirable?"

I said, "Honestly?"

She said, "Does a bear poop in the woods?'

I said, "Okay, fine. You are a virtual jackpot of admirable qualities; you're sexy, the real deal. Not like these anorexic bitches on the cover of *Vogue*. You're a winner on all counts. I can't resist you, and I don't want to, either. Good enough?"

She said, "Wow."

I said, "Wow? What are you, fifteen years old?"

She giggled and said, "I'm beginning to feel like a teenager again, yes."

I said, "But I warn you, I am not a male person, I'm a *man*. And if you expect me to play Prince Charming for you it will have to be on a rented horse. Success has lost my address. I don't have a lot of money."

She said, "And I'm no Princess, either. But if you are looking for *real* love, honesty, and loyalty, you won't have to look any further than apartment three."

I said, "I'll most definitely keep that in mind. Now, shall we get back to business?"

She said, "Yes, sir."

I said, "And don't call me sir. It makes me feel like an old man."

With that sly grin, she said, "Yes, sir."

#

I walked down to the local watering hole around dark, and as I approached the building, I could already see that it was packed with the local drunks, the jukebox blaring some corn pone, cry-a-tear-in-my-beer song, and I knew I had shown up just at the right time.

As I walked in, I could see most of the patrons were already buzzed and formed in groups, the local farmers in one, the local winos in one, the pool sharks in another, and the ladies gathered by the jukebox feeding quarters into it as fast as the songs were playing.

Nobody even noticed me at first.

Good, I thought. That's the way I like it.

Incognito.

So, I sauntered up to the bar like John Wayne, and ordered a beer – and waited.

#

A short time later, slowly but surely, I made my way through the crowd, stopping momentarily to mingle, dropping hints that I was looking for Wade.

To my surprise, even with most of the crowd's tongues loosened up by now, nobody took the bait.

At my wit's end for the time being, I walked back up to the bar and ordered a fresh beer. The bartender, a tall, stocky fellow with military tattoos, a buzz cut hair style, and a big scar over his right eye, brought the beer and whispered, "So, I hear you're looking for Wade Mulley."

I said, "Yeah, with no luck, too."

He said, "I hear you owe him some money, huh?"

I said, "Yeah, over a penny anty poker game, no less. But I'm an honest man."

He said, "Uh huh. Well, I was just curious, because it's usually that Wade owes other people money."

I said, "Like I said, I'm an honest man."

He said, "I bet you are."

I said, "Meaning?"

He said, "Meaning nothing, really. Except for the fact there really aren't all that many honest folks that frequent this establishment. You keep snooping around asking about that asshole, you might find that out the hard way."

I took a big sip of my beer and said, "I'll keep that in mind." I lit a cigarette, drained my beer, and said to the bartender, "Well, friend, thanks for the advice."

As I began to leave, he stopped me, leaned across the bar, and whispered, "You really want to find Wade? Look up a Miss Bobbie Jo Dix, his ex old lady."

I whispered, "And just where might I find Miss Bobbie Jo Dix?"

He said, "She isn't that hard to find. Just hang out in the right places, and you'll find her."

I said, "Which would be?"

He said, "I've said enough already. You have a nice day, *friend*."

Taking the hint, I left post haste.

ELEVEN

By the time I got back to my place, Audrey was sitting on the front porch, with Patty nestled in her lap, purring up a storm.

Walking up to the steps, I said, "Well, if it isn't my two favorite ladies."

Audrey said, "And if it isn't my favorite sleuth. Have any luck?"

I sat down next to her, and I could smell the scents of strawberry shampoo and Chanel number five. After my heart stopped beating a little faster, I said, "Not much luck, no. But the bartender steered me in the right direction."

"How so?" she said, stroking Patty's fur. She purred loudly.

I said, "He told me to look up Wade's ex wife, Bobbi Jo Dix. Have you heard of her before? I didn't see anything about her in your file folder."

She said, "The name doesn't sound familiar, no. How are you supposed to find her?"

I said, "The bartender, he said to just look in the right places, which I gather would mean hanging around more low class establishments, around even more undesirable people."

She said, "That doesn't very healthy."

I said, "No, it doesn't."

She said, "So, what are you going to do?"

I said, "What else? Go look for her."

She said, "Not tonight, I hope. I thought we might just relax on the front porch for a while?"

I said, "Your wish is my command, my lady. How about a cold beer? I know I could use one."

"Yes, please," she said, flashing that beauitful smile.

That's all it took for me.

#

About an hour later, as we sat on the porch sipping beer and gazing up at the stars, with Patty laying close by napping, Audrey had said, "You know, when I was a little girl, I used to sit outside my bedroom window, on the roof, and make wishes on the stars."

Pleasantly surprised, I said, "Me, too. I used to give them names, too."

She said, "Such as?"

I said, "Well, I had Milky Way Street, and the Big Dipper Road. Whenever I felt like I needed to escape my home life – which was more often than not – I would make a wish that I could visit those stars, to get away from everything."

She said, "Oh my, that's sad."

I said, "Well, so was my childhood." I sipped from my beer and said, "But I don't want to talk about that, if you don't mind."

She smiled and said, "Then we won't talk about it. By the way, on more pleasant subjects, I am becoming quite fond of Patty."

I said, "I think she is becoming quite fond of you, too."

Audrey said, "If you like, I can keep an eye on her for you, say, at times you are gone, or catching up on some sleep."

I said, "I think that's a great idea, thank you."

She leaned closer to me and said, "Why the name Patty, by the way? That isn't your typical cat name."

I said, "It's a long story, and to be honest, I really don't want to talk about that, either."

She said, "Done. Now, what shall we talk about, then?"

I cracked a mischievous grin, and said, "Why don't we talk more about those special kisses of yours? I think that's a good subject."

She cracked that sly grin of hers, and said, "Then why don't you lean over here, and get one, you handsome hunk of man?"

I said, "*Hunk*? Well, at least you didn't call me *dude*."

She said, jokingly, "You want a kiss or not?"

I said, "Yes, ma'am."

So we kissed.

For the next half hour or so, we kissed a lot.

An hour later, we were in bed.

TWELVE

Asleep, that is.

Yes, asleep.

Don't get me wrong; I was extremely attracted to Audrey, and hadn't been with a woman in a long time. But, at the same time, I didn't want to ruin a good thing just for the sake of momentary pleasure, adolescent lust in place of real love between two people who had been total strangers to each other until now.

I was playing for *keeps*.

No mind games or one night stands for me.

It was all or nothing.

As it should be.

#

I woke up the next morning around daylight, hearing a loud purring sound and smelling freshly brewed coffee.

I opened my weary eyes to see Patty lying next to me on my pillow, and Audrey sitting on the edge of the bed, holding two steaming cups of fortified coffee.

She smiled and said, jokingly, "Wake up, sleepy head. Breakfast is ready."

I sniffed the air and said, "Smells good and strong."

She said, "I figured you'd need a good strong cup

of coffee after last night."

I said, "Meaning?"

She giggled and said, "Never mind."

I said, "Seriously, was I dreaming again last night?"

She said, "Yes, and tossing and turning."

I said, "Sorry. I do that from time to time."

She said, "What do you dream about, if I may ask?"

I sipped my coffee and said, "Believe me, you don't want to know."

She said, "Fair enough. Sometimes I have bad dreams, too."

I said, "I bet you do. Speaking of which, do you dream about Sherri very often?"

Doing her best to hold back tears, she said, "Yes, I do. And to be completely honest with you, that'e one reason I needed the company last night."

To lighten the mood, I said, jokingly, "Damn. And I thought it was because of my natural good looks and charming personality."

Forcing a smile, she said, "Well, and that, too."

I said, "So, my dear, would you be so kind as to babysit for Patty today?" At the sound of her name being mentioned, Patty curled up next to Audrey, as if she had understood what I'd said.

She said, "Why of course. What's on the agenda for today?"

I said, "I'm going to try and find out the current whereabouts of a Miss Bobbie Dix."

She said, "Do you think that's a good idea after last night?"

I said, "Not really. That's why I'm going to look

her up on the internet."

She said, "Ah, yes, the world wide web. But, how can you find her on the internet?"

I said, "It's easy enough. You can even find digital files of old phone books. It shouldn't be any problem at all."

She sipped her coffee and said, "That sets my mind at ease."

I said, "I thought it would. I didn't want you to worry about me."

She leaned in and kissed me on the cheek, and said, "Thank you my dear."

I said, "You're very welcome, my Princess."

Then she kissed me again.

Needless to say, I was late getting in the shower.

THIRTEEN

It hadn't taken me long to find her.

The old phone book listing was still there:
Roberta J Dix
911 Indiana Avenue
882 / 4082

Knowing the number was most likely from an old now defunct land line, I just wrote the postal address down and put it in my pocket.

Audrey was sitting on the porch with Patty on her lap, soaking up the sun, and upon seeing me, Audrey said, "I'll hold down the fort while you're gone. Me and Patty, that is."

I said, "Thank you my dear. I promise I won't be long."

She said, "You better not be, mister. I might need another kiss."

I said, "In that case, I will try to my trip extra fast."

As I turned to walk down the front steps, Audrey said, "Chuck?"

I said, "Yes my dear?"

She said, "Please, be careful."

"I promise," I said, already wishing I was staying home instead, but I had already made a promise.

Bobbie Dix's old postal address wasn't more than half a mile away, so it hadn't taken me long to get there.

The neighborhood she lived in – or used to live in, possibly – was what most folks in Wabash would refer to as "the wrong side of the tracks."

Derelict houses and weatherbeaten trailers lined both sides of the street, along with piles of trash bags and other discarded items that had once upon a time, held some kind of importance for someone, but not any more.

I found her old address quickly; an old, one story home that had been a cute little place long ago, with a decent flower garden, but just like most homes in that section of town, was now old, dilapidated, and in dire need of repair.

I walked up to the front door, past an old discarded washing machine and an old car engine, to the outside screen door, which was full of holes and barely hanging on by the door frame.

I took a deep breath, exhaled, and knocked on the outside door. After a few moments had gone by with no answer, I gently opened the outside door, and this time, knocked harder, on the inside door.

Then I knocked again.

Within a few seconds, I could hear someone moving around in there, not walking, but *stomping* toward the front door, and cursing under their breath.

A moment later, the door opened, and short, stocky woman with grey hair who had definitely seen the better side of fifty, said, "Yeah?"

I said, "Excuse me, ma'am, but I'm looking for a Miss Bobbie Dix?"

Studying my face, she said, "That's me. And you are?"

"Chuck Polanski," I said, forcing a smile. "I'm an old friend of Wade Mulley."

Looking me over once again, she said, "Well, I know all of his so called "friends," and you, mister, ain't one of them."

Normally quick on my feet, I smiled and said, "Well, I knew him way back when, in highschool."

Equally quick with a comeback, she said, "I knew all of his goofy school buddies, too, and you ain't one of them. Who the hell are you, really?"

Realizing that I had met my match with another person of plenty of street smarts, I just came out with the truth and said, "I represent a lady who believes that your ex husband might have been involved in the *murder* of her daughter. Does that ring a bell?"

If looks could kill, I would have been a dead man that day. I could see the muscles in her neck tighten up, and her beady little eyes fixed on mine as she said, "Who *are* you, you old prick?"

I said, "I told you who I was. And, if you don't answer my questions, I'll just turn this matter over to the local yokel cops, who most likely won't be as polite as I am."

She moved forward, reached out, and slammed the screen door open so hard, it almost came loose from the hinges, and said, "Listen here, you old turd. You're talking about *old* news. He didn't do jack shit to that girl, and neither did I. You'd best stop this nonsense, and move on, before *you* end up getting hurt."

I said, politely as possible, "Miss Dix, did you just *threaten* me?"

She said, "That wasn't a threat, you old shit, that was a *promise*."

I stepped forward then, calling her bluff, and said, "You know what I think?"

Stepping back, almost tripping over her own feet, she said, "Who gives a shit what you think?"

I said, "You better give a shit, because here is what I think; back in seventy five, you and your psycho hubby were out on a joy ride, ran across Sherri and her boyfriend, and you beat the shit out of him, stuffed him in his own trunk to smother to death, then proceeded to take Sherri to that horse barn for a little party."

Bobbie Dix went ballistic then, wavng her arms in the air and screaming. She pointed her finger at me and said, "You son of a bitch! You're crazy! Get off of my property before I *kill* you!"

I stood back then, cracked a big grin, and said, "Now, there is the *real* Bobbie Dix. You have a good day now, Miss Dix. I'm sure we'll talk again soon enough."

As I turned to leave, she walked up behind me, screaming and cursing and waving her fists in the air.

I just kept on walking – and grinning – all the way home.

FOURTEEN

When I got back home, Audrey and Patty were still sitting on the front porch, patiently awaiting my return.

After my not so pleasant visit with Bobbie Dix, I was very glad to see my two favorite ladies.

As I sat down on the top step to catch my breath, Audrey said, "So, I gather your visit didn't go so well?"

I said, "Is it that obvious?"

She said, "It's in the eyes. What happened?"

I lit a cigarette and said, "Well, she threatened to *kill* me, if I didn't vacate her property poste haste."

Audrey said, "Well, if there ever was a sign of guilt – and the propensity for violence – I'd say she wins hands down."

I said, "She's as dirty as dogshit, and I bet good old Wade is, too."

Before Audrey could reply, a familiar Sedan pulled up out front again, and she said, "Oh no, not this early in the day."

I stood to my feet and said, "Don't worry, he won't be here long."

By that tme Crow had already goose-stomped up to the steps like a Nazi, stopped right in front of me, and, with his hands fumbling nervously through his jacket pockets, he said, "Do you actually *enjoy* spending time in jail?"

I said, "Do you have something interesting in your pocket, or are you just glad to see me?"

Crow said, "As usual, the comedian."

I said, "I try."

Crow said, "Why don't you ever try taking good advice for a change?"

Already tiring of the conversation, I said, "Crow, if you have something to say, just say it. I'm really not in the mood for your bullshit."

Before he could retort, Audrey spoke up and said, "Mr Crow, I must agree. What is it you have against Mr Polanski?"

Crow said, "Believe me, ma'am, it is nothing personal. I'm just doing my job."

Stroking Patty's fur, Audrey said, "Is part of your job making his life – and *my* life – as miserable as possible?"

He said, "No, it isn't."

I said, "Well, you're doing a hell of a good job of it, Crow. Miss Gibson doesn't deserve this, either."

Crow lit a cigarette and said, "Yes, I know. I've read up on the case, and to be honest, it's just as cold as it was back then."

Audrey said, "Hence Mr Polanksi's assistance in solving the case."

Crow said, "I'm trying to keep him from getting hurt – or worse."

I said, "I can take care of myself, Crow. You know that by now."

He said, "This is true. But, hanging around a bar full of his old buddies, dropping hints, is a good way to end up with a knife in your guts."

I said, "Or vise versa."

Crow said, "Exactly. Either way, you could end up in the county jail, or in the county morgue."

I said, "I'll take my chances."

He said, "Fine. It's your ass, not mine."

As Crow turned to leave, Audrey said, "And Mr Crow?"

Crow stopped and said, "Yes?"

She said, "Why don't you go screw yourself?"

#

After Crow left, Audrey wasn't the same.

She just sat there in her lawn chair, stroking Patty's fur, listening to her purr, and staring out at nothing at all. Her eyes were empty, void of any real emotion.

I stood up, sat down next to her, grasped her hand gently in my own, and said, "Penny for your thoughts?"

She forced a smile and said, "I just hate that asshole, that's all. He's nothing more to me than yet another painful reminder of exactly why this case has never been solved."

I said, "I must agree."

She said, "But I have you, to help me, don't I?"

I said, "And always will."

She managed to crack a smile then, and said, "Thank you my Prince."

I said, "You are very welcome, my Princess."

She said, "So, what's on the agenda for the rest of the day?"

I said, "Anything you'd like."

She said, "How about another little porch picnic?"

I said, "That sounds great. I'll take a walk down to

the corner market, and pick up a few things."

She said, "Okie dokie. While you're there, would you mind picking up some more cigarettes and single malt? I think I'm going to need it."

"Me too," I said. "Me, too."

FIFTEEN

While Audrey gave Patty some tuna platter and swept off the front porch, I had taken a stroll down to the market for some picnic supplies.

While I strolled through the aisles, picking out the obligatory picnic supplies – chips, dip, lunchmeat, bread, and smokes – I was suddenly startled by a deep, raspy voice coming up behind me.

I turned to see a tall, stocky, heavily tattooed man of around sixty years old, dressed in tye dye t -shirt and faded blue jeans. He looked like a reject from the Summer of love, the hippy generation, although I kept my opinion to myself.

I said, "Come again?"

He said, "I said, did you ever find Wade? I heard you've been looking for him."

I said, "Nope, no luck so far. Why do you ask, friend?"

He snickered and said, "I ain't no friend of yours, asshole. But I will give you some friendly advice."

"Which is?" I said, backing up a step or two.

He said, "Best stop snooping around where you ain't welcome, dipshit. It could be hazardous to your health."

I said, "I'll keep that in mind. Anything else?"

Turning to walk away, the big goon said, "For

now, no. Best keep it that way, too."

I nodded my understanding, and he turned away and disppeared into the crowd. I stood there for a few moments, making sure he was gone, then resumed my little shopping expedition, the whole time thinking about my promise to Audrey – and, if I was going to be alive long enough to fulfill it.

#

I didn't bother telling Audrey about the incident at the market.

I walked up on the front porch, carrying the picnic goodies, to see her and Patty sitting in the lawn chair again, Patty purring up a storm and Audrey freshly showered, wearing a sundress and sandals and another small sunflower tucked behind one ear.

She knew what I liked, and made sure I recieved it. She always made sure I was happy, no matter if she felt up to it or not, and that's the moment I decided I must do the same thing, not only because I had made a promise, but because it was just the *right* thing to do.

And, I felt like I was falling in love with her, too.

She said, "So, what are we having for our porch picnic today?"

Setting the bags down on the porch, I said, "How about chicken salad sandwiches, chips, and sun tea?"

She said, "Yummy. And for dessert?"

I said, "Some single malt?"

She smiled and said, "Perfect."

I said, "Coming right up!"

#

After our picnic, as we sat on the porch, sipping single malt, watching Patty play with one of her catnip toys, and generally just enjoying the moment, my mind kept drifting back to the fact I felt as though I was falling for her, and, at the same time, my fear of rejection.

I knew she cared a lot for me; that fact was all too apparent. But, would she share the same feelings I felt for her? And if not, would I scare her away by telling her how I felt about her?

That thought, for me, was actually more terrifying than telling her I was falling in love with her.

So, as I sat here sipping my single malt, I'd decided to keep my feelings a secret for now – but knew I couldn't keep it a secret for much longer.

I said, "There's that look in your eyes again. May I ask what is on your mind, my dear?"

She cracked that little sly little grin of hers again, and said, "What look is that?"

I said, "That look you get when you are trying to make me guess what you're thinking about."

She giggled and said, "Okay, you got me. I was thinking about making you guess what I'm thinking about."

"Which is?" hoping to hear something pleasant – and promising.

She said, "Well, I've been missing our sweet little kisses today. An old gal like me can only go so long without some good hugs and smooches, you know."

Scooting my chair closer, I said, "Your wish is my command, my lady." Then I kissed her.

She kissed me back.

Then we kissed again.

Afterward, as we sat gazing into each other's eyes, she said, "A penny for *your* thoughts?"

I said, "Are you *sure* you want to know?"

She said, "I wouldn't have asked otherwise, silly boy."

I couldn't hold back any longer. I said, "I think I'm falling in love with you." *There, I did it. Now for the rejection and heartache.*

She just sat there for a few seconds, her mouth hanging wide open in awe, and then she cleared her throat and said, "I thought it was just *me*."

I couldn't believe my ears, as I said, "You feel the same way?"

With tears of joy streaming from her eyes, she said, "Oh yes, I was just afraid you wouldn't feel the same way."

I said, "Me too!"

At that moment, without another word exchanged, we fell into each other's arms, hugging each other so tight we thought our hearts would explode.

As she pulled away, looking into my eyes, she said, "Well, where do we go from here, my love?"

I said, "I say we celebrate. The heck with porch picnics. Tomorrow night, we eat at a real restaurant."

She gave me one of those good kisses of hers, and said, "Does this mean we are engaged?"

I said, jokingly, "That depends on whether you like Goodwill grade engagement rings, but otherwise, I guess so."

She giggled and said, "That's good enough for me, as long as I'm with you."

So, we were engaged.

SIXTEEN

Or, as engaged as we were going to be, anyway.

But it was good enough for us.

I had logged into my computer, looking up nearby restaurants, and Audrey had picked Applebee's. Which was fine by me, they had a great looking bourbon burger.

Me and my bourbon; what can I say?

#

The next evening, we arrived at Applebee's around dusk, and, to our delight, found a booth facing the big bay window in front, so we could watch the sunset together as we ate our dinner.

It had been, so far, the proverbial perfect evening for two people in love.

As we sat eating our dinner – me with my big juicy bourbon burger and draft beer, and Audrey nibbling on her pasta salad and sipping red wine – I said, "So, how's the food? Is it satisfactory for my lady?"

She said "Oh yes, very much so. I don't need anything fancy to be happy."

"Me neither," I said, sipping my beer.

She said, "It beats eating a bowl of greasy chili at

the neighborhood bar."

I said, "You got that shit right."

She said, "Speaking of which, would you do me a favor?"

"Anything, my love," I said, and meant it.

She said, "Stay away from that bar down the street. I don't think it's going to be good for your health."

I said, "Already thought about it, and I intend to steer clear of it in the future."

"Thank you," she said, flashing me a playful wink. "So, after dinner, why don't we sit on the front porch, and play kissy-face like a couple of horny teenagers?"

Raising my beer in a toast to the occasion, I said, "Sounds great to me, it's a date."

As we sat there for a little while longer, enjoying our dinner – but mainly each other's company – we had no idea at the time that our date night would soon be turned upside down.

#

When we arrived back home, and entered the building, I noticed right away that my apartment door was hanging wide open.

Before I could say a word, she said, "Oh my God, Chuck. Now what?"

I said, "Just stay behind me."

I slowly, cautiously, walked into my apartment, my mind wired tight and my fists balled up, ready for a good fight if need be.

But there was nobody in there, except for Patty,

who was lying under the kitchen table, shivering with fright.

As I leaned down to pick her up, I glanced around to see nothing was out of place, or broken, etc.

But when my eyes fixed upon my computer desk, I could see that Audrey's file folder was missing.

Whoever came in here was doing so for a specific reason, and it wasn't to rob me.

It was to steal any evidence that Audrey had put together over the last few decades.

I could only think of two specific people who would have wanted to steal it too; Bobbie Dix or Wade Mulley.

Audrey was behind me then, saying, "Well, is anything missing?"

I said, "One thing only; your file folder."

She said, "Oh no! Not my folder!" I could tell by the look in her eyes, on her face, her heart was broken – all over again. I placed Patty on the floor at my feet, and hugged Audrey, trying to console her, but she was beyond consoling at the time.

We stood there in the kitchen for the next several minutes, her tears flowing like rain, until her tears ran dry. The whole time, I was thinking about how much I wanted to get my hands on Bobbi or Wade, wrap my fingers around their throat, and choke the very life out of them.

But I had to keep myself together for Audrey's ake – and my own, if I didn't want to end up in jail.

SEVENTEEN

Believe it or not, I called the police to report the robbery.

Believe it or not, the cop that showed up to take the report was none other than my favorite Detective, Harley Crow.

As he arrived, walking in to find Audrey and I sitting at the kitchen table, smoking cigarettes and sipping fortified coffee, he just stood there in the doorway and said, "Well, Mr Polanksi. What have we gotten ourselves into this time?"

I said, "Please, save the smartass remarks for now, I'm not in the mood."

Crow said, "Yeah? Me neither. I was on my way home to eat some homemade meatloaf, when I heard about this call over my car radio, and I said to myself, no, don't go over there, go home and eat my dinner. But for some reason, I couldn't resist seeing what you've done this time."

I said, "I haven't done anything, asshole. Some other asshole broke in and stole something very important."

Audrey said, "Yes, *very* imortant, Mr Crow."

Lighting a cigarette, Crow said, "And just what was so important for someone to want to break into this dump?"

I said, "A file folder."

Crow said, "And? What was in the file folder?"

Audrey said, sarcastically, "Oh, not much. Only about thirty years worth of information about my daughter's murder – and the name of one of the suspects."

Crow said, "Yes, I know. Mr Wade Mulley. Like I've said before, we didn't have enough on him to charge him with anything."

I said, "You would have had enough, if someone hadn't stole it."

Audrey said, "So, what are you going to do about this, Mr Crow?"

He said, "I want to tell you both something, in confidence, that is."

I said, "We're listening."

"Your daughter's case? It's still *open*."

Audrey stood up and said, "What?! Then why haven't you done anything about it?"

Crow said, "It's a *cold case*, that's still open, if that makes any sense."

I said, "No, it doesn't make any sense. Please, enlighten us as to your plans for this case."

Crow said, "We were afraid if we brought this case out into the open again too soon, it would scare the guilty party away. As it is, Mulley is more or less a transcient, moves around a lot."

Sitting back down, Audrey said, "Which means, he has most likely hurt – or killed – even *more* young women over the years. Great job, Mr Crow."

Crow said, "I'm sorry, ma'am. But I do my best with what I'm allowed to work with."

I said, "So, now what? That file folder could have

been a big help with your investigation."

Crow said, "True, but, we have a file folder of our own, too."

Audrey said, "And? Do you intend to use it?"

Crow said, "We already have."

I said, "And?"

Crow said, "We have intel that Wade is back in town now, and has been keeping in touch with Bobbi. We have eyes on her place twenty-four-seven."

Audrey said, "Now that *is* good news."

I said, "Well, Crow. I hate to admit this, but I might have judged you prematurely."

Cracking a smile, Crow said, "It's okay, Polanski. It's not the first time, and I'm sure it won't be the last time, either."

Audrey said, "So, now what?"

Crow said, "Now, you and your boyfriend here are to lay *low*, keep out of sight."

I said, "Fine by me."

Audrey said, "Me too."

Crow said, "Great. Now, I'll keep you up on things, so for now, just let me contact you with any new developments."

With that, Crow turned to leave, and I said, "Hey, Crow."

He turned back to me and said, "Yeah, I know. Go screw myself."

I said, "Actually, I was going to say thanks for the help, but if you really want to screw yourself, it's fine by me."

Crow said, "Well, screw you too, Polanski," cracked a big grin, and walked out.

EIGHTEEN

So, for the next few weeks, we did just that.

Not screw ourselves, mind you, but laid low and kept out of sight – except for our porch picnics.

We would spend our days on the porch, enjoying the sunshine, and when a rain cloud would open itself up above us, she would frown, thinking of only the things lost to them. I knew at times she'd spend more time longing for things we couldn't have, and longing for what had been ripped from our grasp unfairly.

Like the return of her daughter, or my past slate wiped clean.

Wiping those tears away she'd look for me and find me watching, waiting, my arms open, and a word of comfort on my lips. Holding tightly to each was how we'd watch the sunsets, my hands in her hair and her head on my chest.

As long as we had each other, we made it through somehow.

#

One sunny day, we had been sitting on the porch being entertained by watching Patty chase a squirrel when Audrey has said, "You know, it was day exactly like this, when Sherri and I last spent time together."

I said, "That's a good memory then."

She forced a smile and said, "Yes, it is. You know, we should take a walk to the cemetery, and place some fresh flowers on her grave today."

I said, "That sounds like a wonderful idea."

She said, "It's been a while since I was there, you know, because of this open case and all."

I said, "Well, under the circumstances, I am sure Sherri would understand."

She said, "Yes, but I *need* this, Chuck, and you know that."

I said, "Then visit Sherri we shall do."

So we did.

#

Audrey was right; it was the perfect day for a walk to the cemetery.

The cemetery, normally, would be considered a sad place, one of a somber mood and tears and mourning.

But that day, with the abundant sunshine and the birds singing in the trees and the fact we were there *together*, made it all more bearable.

As we stood by Sherri's grave, and Audrey placed the fresh roses on the headstone, she stood back and said, "Chuck, do you believe in Heaven and hell?"

I said, "I do now. If there wasn't a Heaven, and God, an ornery old fart like me would have been roasting on a spicket in hell by now."

She said, "I hope you're right. If anyone ever deserved to be in Heaven, it's my Sherri."

I grasped her hand gently in my own, and said,

"I'm sure she is, and is smiling down on you right now, so proud of you for keeping her memory alive, and never giving up."

Squeezing my hand gently, she said, "Thank you Chuck. And you most definitely have a way with words."

I said, "I try."

She said, "Your efforts have definitely not been in vain."

Looking up at the beautiful ocean blue sky, I said, "You know, when we leave here, we should take a walk down to the corner market, and grab some porch picnic supplies."

Her face lit up as she said, "Can we have salami and swiss?! You know how much I love your salami and swiss sandwiches."

"Salami and swiss it is," I said, as we turned to leave. We hadn't walked more than a few feet away from Sherri's grave when Audrey stopped, turned around, and said, "Don't worry, Sherri, I'm in good hands, now."

Then she kissed me.

One of her *special* kisses.

I was in good hands now, too.

NINETEEN

When we arrived back home, Patty was still chasing squirrels up a tree.

Upon seeing us, though, she had abandoned her quest and scampered over to greet us, purring up a storm.

Audrey picked her up and we all took our usual spots on the front porch, as I unpacked the food and opened the wine.

A few minutes later, as Audrey and I sat eating our sandwiches and sipping red wine, I couldn't help but wonder how Crow was coming along with the case, but kept my thoughts to myself. Audrey was currently in a good mood, and she deserved to stay that way for now.

I couldn't help but think of that day she had almost teetered over the edge, too. She'd almost gone over the edge of *sanity*, that day, because of her vulnerability.

But I had been there to save her, as I would always be in the future. She had saved my life – and sanity too – so I owed her the same.

As Patty sat on Audrey's lap, doing her best to bum a piece of salami, Audrey smiled and said, "I can't really think of a day, in such a long time, I've felt this happy, and blessed."

I knew the feeling all too well. I said, "I feel the

same way, my love, and I owe it all to you."

She flashed me that sly little grin of hers, and said, "You better watch it, or I'll smother you with some more of my special kisses."

I said, "Then I'll be sure to be a naughty boy for the rest of the day."

She grinned, and looked upward toward the sky, as if in deep thought, and said, "You know, I never had stopped to think about it until now, that the lights up in the sky, have to be billions of years old by the time we see it, from the beginning of time right past us, into the future."

I said, "Maybe they're souls, traveling through starlight, searching for homes."

She said, "I've already *found* my home."

Flashing her a playful little wink, I said, "Me, too."

Patty finally managed to steal a piece of salami, and Audrey giggled and placed her on the porch at her feet, and said, "Shall we watch the sunset later? I bet it's going to be a special one."

"My thoughts exactly," I said, leaning in closer to her chair. "But first, some of those special smooches?"

Leaning in too, she said, "Your wish is my command, my Prince."

That was our life again for weeks on end, not that we were complaining, of course.

TWENTY

But after so many weeks went by again, Audrey had begun feeling hopeless again, about the case being solved any time soon, and I had to admit, I had felt the same way.

As usual, though, we managed to muddle through it all somehow.

#

Then one day, toward the end of August, as we sat on the front porch watching Patty chase her tail, Audrey had poured her black coffee out on the ground, and said, "May I have some fortified coffee now, my dear? This black coffee just isn't doing the trick."

Feeling the same way at the time, I'd said, "Me too. Coming right up."

After I had fortified our coffee, we sat there sipping and smoking and sipping some more, until we finally felt as though we were on an even keel again, which in all reality wasn't a good thing.

We had spent almost two months getting our lives back together – becoming a couple – and now we were allowing our impatience over the case to get the best of us all over again.

That is, until the day Crow finally showed up –

and with good news, this time.

#

We had been sitting on the front porch, as usual, sipping our fortified coffee and doing our best to avoid chatting about anything depressing, when that old familiar Sedan pulled up out front, and Crow climbed out, wearing a big smile, and carrying a file folder.

By the time he reached the porch, I was already on my feet, saying, "Well?"

Audrey was on her feet too, her hands trembling as she sipped her coffee. She said, "Please, give us good news, Mr Crow."

Crow handed me the file folder, and said, "I thought you'd want this back. We've made copies of it all, so no worries."

It was Audrey's file folder.

She walked over to me, with tears in her eyes, and snatched the folder right out of my hands, cradling it against her chest, against her heart.

She said to Crow, "Where did you find it?"

Crow said, "At the motel room, where we arrested Wade Mulley for first degree murder."

I said, "What?!"

Crow said, "Believe it or not, his ex wife, Bobbie Dix, walked into police headquarters day before yesterday, and made a full confession about her role in the crime. Then we staked out Wade's motel room over in Knox County, and arrested him when he walked outside to smoke a cigarette."

With tears in her eyes, Audrey said, "So, it's really all over now? My Sherri can rest in peace?"

Crow said, "Thanks to your boyfriend here."

I said, "Come again?"

Crow said, "She said that after you paid her a visit, she sat around for weeks and weeks, with the guilt eating away at her like a cancer. She couldn't take it any more, and confessed."

I said, proudly, "See, Crow? Your pain in the ass did a good thing, didn't I?"

Crow grinned and said, "Yes, you did, Polanski. But in the future..."

I said, "Yeah, I know. Keep my ass away from your crime scenes."

He said, jokingly, "Yeah, for now, any way."

He turned to leave and I said, "Hey, Crow."

He stopped, and said, "Yeah?"

I said, "All those times I told you to go screw yourself? I was just kidding around."

He grinned and said, "Really? Because I wasn't."

Then he was gone.

I silently wished for him to kiss my ass.

TWENTY ONE

After that day, it was like Audrey was finally whole again.

She woke up each day looking forward to enjoying the day to it's fullest, and I felt the same way, knowing that her precious daughter could rest in peace now, and that Audrey was happy – *really* happy – for the first time in decades.

Just like I was, too.

Then, right out the blue, my cancer came back again, with a vengeance.

#

But I needn't have worried about going through it alone, this time.

To my surprise, Audrey stuck with my stubborn old ass through it all, watching over me, and my kitty, and was always there when I needed her to make me feel better.

Just like I'd been there for her, but never really expected her to repay the favor. Her just being in my life was payment enough.

Five months later, to my utter surprise, I was told by my onocologist I was in remission again.

I didn't waste one single moment after that.

Myself and Audrey and Patty became totally inseperable, and spent every waking moment living our lives to the fullest, and it was the happiest time of our lives.

Yeah, I know.

Did I still drink?

Sometimes, yes, but not like I used to drink. I didn't have any empty voids left to fill.

Neither did Audrey.

So we filled our hearts with love.

Love...the thing I used to think was a lie, a trap, to torture poor suckers like myself.

But now, not so much.

Now, when I lay down at night, I sleep with an angel by my side. What more could a poor lost soul like me ask for?

Amen.

Afterword

The character of Chuck Polanski is based on myself, and my years as an alcoholic and aspiring writer. I have been sober now for seventeen years.

The character of Audrey is based on Sherri Gibson's real mother, who has sadly passed way, but can now rest in peace.

The character of Wade Mulley is based on Wayne Gulley, the man who helped to murder Sherri Gibson. He is now serving sixty years in prison.

He will *die* in prison.

The character of Bobbie Dix is based on Ella Mae Dicks, Gulley's girlfiend at the time of the crime. She too is now serving time in prison, and will most likely die there, too.

David Boyer is a Christian, a multi-genre writer, a true crime buff, and the author of several coming of age novellas, numerous horror and scifi stories, as well as the author of numerous essays including the subjects of government corruption, Christianity, bullying, and cyber-stalking.

He lives in Vincennes, Indiana, with his cat, Holly Jean, who now serves as his copy editor by jumping on the computer keyboard when he's not looking.

Books: {Non-fiction}
True crime:
Small Town Murder: True Crime Stories From Knox County, Indiana
Murder In the Hoosier Heartland: Infamous Indiana Murderers & Fledgling Serial Killers
Murder & Mayhem In the Hoosier Heartland: Mysterious Disappearances & Bizarre Murders In Indiana
The Blitz: A Rape Victim's Story
Vanished In Vincennes: the Mysterious Disappearance and Death Of Dolores Oliver
47 Years of Hell: The Dolores Oliver Murder: Still Unsolved
Small Town Murder In Knox County, Indiana: Hate Crimes, Witch Hunts, and A Definitive List of Indiana Serial Killers
The Guy In The Blue Shirt

Non-fiction: {paranormal, bio & memoir}
Haunted Heartland: Haunted Hoosiers Tell Their Ghost Stories
Strange Happenings In the Hoosier Heartland
I Remember When, In Vincennes...Volume 1
Growing Up In Vincennes – Volumes 2 – 5
The Time of Our Lives: Growing Up Cool In Vincennes, Indiana

Essays:
Bullying: the Road to Recovery and Forgiveness
Privacy In the Age of the Internet: How Sexting and Sharing Private Photos Can lead To Cyber-Stalking

Once An Alcoholic, Always An Alcoholic? The Cold Hard Truth About Our Addictions
Travesties of Jutice: Flaws In Our Legal System That Imprison the Innocent
Will the REAL Christian Please Stand Up?
Racism in the 21ˢᵗ Century: ALL Lives Matter
Conflicted Souls: How the Man In Black Saved My Life
Crossing the Rainbow Bridge: Saying Goodbye To Our Beloved Pets

Books: {Fiction}
Mystery, Indiana
Human Sawdust

Stories: {Long fiction, novellas}
Mystery, Indiana
The Mind of Luther Biggs
LUTHER
Jenny
Lester Talbot and His Magic Eye
Beautiful Ghosts
Pretty Flamingo
Jack and Norma Jean
The Things We Leave Behind – Volumes 1 – 3
Ghosts of Summer
Gardens
Claustrophobia
The Cemetery Artist
Brain Pie
Beast
The Jailhouse Movie Star
Easy Pickings
The Dominant Thumb
Joyride
The Maverick
Freak
Grandma's Gooseberry Pie
Dancing With the King

Always In My Heart
Hillbilly Moonshine Zombies
Home
Sheva
A Debt Repaid In Full
The Enlightening Darkness
The Good Neighbor
Wander
The Hungry Ones
A Gunfighter's Legacy
Dead Man's Hand
Inhuman Experiments – Part 1, 2, and 3
Jennifer
Spider Bait
Goodnight, My Love
Poor Larry
Creepy Crawl
The Ballad Of Georgie

Dolores Oliver, fondly nick-named 'Lert' by her friends as a term of endearment, was out an out-going and friendly woman who was well liked by all who knew her.

Yet, on September 7, 1974, while on a visit to a local bar to chat with friends, she simply vanished without a trace. Foul play was immediately suspected by her family, who knew in their hearts that they could think of absolutely no one who would want to do her any harm.

Yet her lifeless body was found at the end of October in a bean field by a farmer in Illinois. Lawrence County coroner Dale Nichols was able to make a positive ID through dental records and a ring Mrs Oliver was wearing.

Who would have done such a thing, and why? Hopefully, VANISHED IN VINCENNES will help to finally solve one of the oldest cold cases in Indiana, and bring her family some closure they have sought for so long.

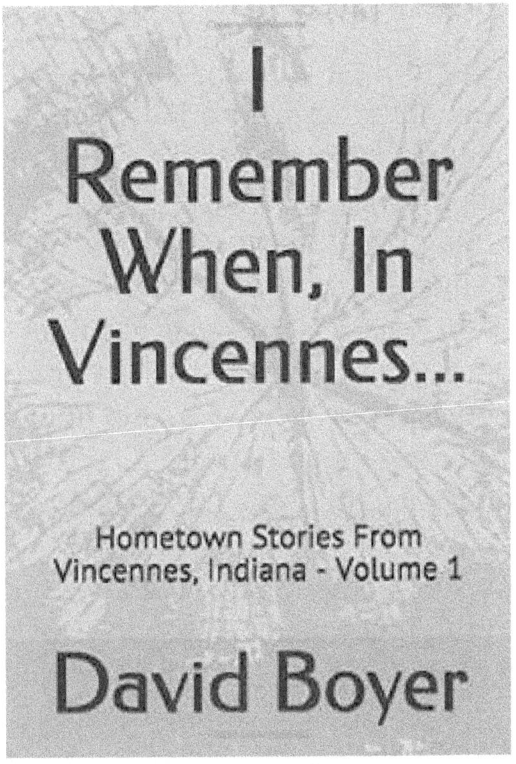

Unfortunately, even small towns – Vincennes included – eventually change, sometimes for the better, and other times, not so much. It's the natural order of things.

Trees grow old and fall. Sidewalks split and crack and are replaced for public safety's sake. Old houses – and all the memories associated with them – are demolished and replaced with parking lots or duplexes. Even historical landmarks, Mother Nature and Father Time having taken their toll, sadly, vanish – except for our own pictures and memories of them.

Luckily for Vincennes residents, local historian Norbert Brown has created a Facebook group page entitled, *Vincennes Remember When*, to help all of us keep our fond memories intact, and to reminisce and enjoy them 24-7.

It was his infinite wisdom of our local history and group page that was the inspiration for this book – and the stories within. Some of these stories may elicit a tear, some laughter.

Some may remind you of an old friend you haven't seen since high school – or, sadly, one that has passed in recent years. Some may remind you of your childhood, your teenage years – or having to bid them farewell, in order to move on to bigger and better things; marriage, children, grandchildren, and a lifetime of wonderful memories that only a tight-knit, loving family can provide.

It is my sincere belief that there will be a story for *everybody* within these pages, regardless of whether you may be a Vincennes history buff or not.

As of 2015, it is believed that there are at least 200 serial killers active in the United States at any given time.

33 of them were from Indiana.

Nobody in their own home town would have wanted to imagine a fledgling {or full fledged} serial killer lurking about, searching for his next victim. Or imagine one being their next door neighbor or the relative of a friend or even attending the local college.

Yet, since the early 1970s, Vincennes, Indiana, Knox County, and Indiana in general has had it's share of cold blooded murder.

It's really sad – as well as terrifying – to even imagine all these brutal, cold blooded murders have taken place in small town communities, where, at one time, we could all trust just about everyone we met at least to the extent they'd do us no harm; a time when could leave our doors unlocked at night or a window open for a cool breeze or not have to worry about where our children were – or if they'd ever come home again.

In SMALL TOWN MURDER, we will be examining local cases, old cases, more recent cases, and the aftermath it leaves behind for the victim's families – as well as taking an in-depth look into a deep, dark, world none of us would ever want to see – but has been here all along, and, most likely, always will be.

Excerpts from the book
The Pearl City Blues
A Chuck Polanski Novel
By
David Boyer

Sometimes you climb out of bed in the morning
and you think, I'm not going to make it, but you
laugh inside – remembering all the times you've
felt that way.

- Charles Bukowski

ONE

It was like any other day in my sad little life.

Up at dawn, two beers and a shot of single malt, then a long hot shower before sitting down at my computer to hopefully come up with something worth reading.

Like I said, just like any other day.

#

Or I'd thought so at the time.

As the day went on, it was much more than a tad bit eventful.

First of all, I had ended up with a case of the dreaded writer's block. Then, to make matter much worse, I'd run out of single malt.

It was time for a trip to the liquor store, post haste.

On the way there, I'd become quite thirsty, and had dropped by the neighborhood tavern for a cold beer.

Bud's tavern was normally a pleasant atmosphere.

After the owners and other patrons got used to seeing you, it was like you were a member of their family. It sort of reminded me of that old TV show, *Cheers*, where, as the title song says, "everybody knows your name."

Each time I walked in the door, there were the

same friendly faces and smiles waiting for me, as well as the obligatory ribbing and joking. Considering the fact I had recently gone through a divorce and a particularly messy breakup as well, Bud's had been the perfect place to escape my lonely, hum-drum lifestyle and make some new friends.

Every Thursday, Friday, and Saturday nights, I could most likely be found sitting at the bar and sipping a cold draft beer and chowing down on some great fried chicken and listening to the jukebox and laughing and cracking jokes and in general just having the time of my life.

It wasn't just the great food and cold beer and all the laughs, either. I used to think that if you had seen one tavern you'd seen them all, but with Bud's, it felt different somehow.

That is, until *that* day.

TWO

When I walked into the tavern that morning, the overall atmosphere was much different than usual.

As soon as I walked in, missing was the usual cheerful banter and laughter, and had been replaced with a air of nervousness and forboding. And, in the middle of it all, sat Mr Dallas Gentry.

Dallas Gentry was born in Pearl City, Indiana, a small, run down community of ramshackle houses and derelict trailers nestled in between the town levee and the Wabash River basin. His mother, Lula, a known alcoholic and brawler, had once sold Dallas in exchange for a carton of cigarettes and a half gallon of whiskey. The woman who'd purchased Dallas had brought him back within two days claiming he wasn't even smart enough to pull a plow or bait a fish hook, and demanded her payment back.

His childhood had been less than pleasant or normal in any way at all.

And it was showing today.

When I walked in, the *only* voice I heard was that of Mr Wallace, loud and boisterous and obviously *drunk*.

As he sat at the bar, gulping down draft beers and regaling the other patrons with tales of his latest escapades – cashing in almost forty-five dollars worth of aluminum cans earlier in the day – everyone else in the place seemed almost entranced by his tale, when, in reality, they were more in fear of him than interested in anything he had to say.

I had to admit, he was a tough looking old fart; big bug eyes, a scarred face, and a deep, raspy voice that sent shivers down your spine whenever he would raise his voice another octave or two.

But his eyes were the most noticeable part of his features.

They seemed to bug out of his head like two hard boiled eggs, bloodshot and empty. When he looked at you, you couldn't tell if he was looking straight at you or past you, or over the top of your head.

It was very creepy to say the least.

#

Anyway, back to the story.

As I walked in, everyone at the bar turned to look at me, flashed me a weak smile, and went back to listening to Dallas brag about his big cash windfall.

I sat at the bar, ordered a beer, and sat listening to him as well, and it hadn't taken me long to get tired of it.

I don't mind listening to someone telling the tall tale – it comes with the territory in a tavern – but, after so long, the *same* story gets tiresome, and I had come in there to *relax*.

After listening to his tale – for the third time in a row – I couldn't take it anymore.

It wasn't because I was jealous of his new found fortune, mind you. I just didn't see any point in repeating the same story over and over again.

I drained my beer, stood up, and calmly walked

around the bar to face him, and said, "Excuse me, sir, but don't you have any *other* stories you can tell? I'm sure you have other tales of drunkenness and ignorance you can entertain us with."

He wheeled around in his barstool, looked me directly in the eyes, and said, "What did you say, you little shit?"

Doing my best to ignore his creepy gaze, I said, "I said, your story is becoming *very* boring, and I came in here to *relax*, not listen to your drunken ramblings all day."

At that very moment, you could have heard a pin drop. The other patrons seemed to gasp for breath, at my bravery – or stupidity, in their eyes.

Dallas said, "If you don't like what I'm talking about, why don't you just get the hell out of here, before I have to stomp your ass?"

Giving him the once over, sizing him up, I could see he had a large hunting knife in a sheath on his ancient leather belt, and I couldn't help but wonder just how many men he'd sliced up with it in the past.

I wasn't going to take any chances.

I forced a smile, extended my hand, and said, "I was just joking, my friend. Please, carry on with your story. I find it quite interesting."

He studied my face for a few moments, he forced a smile and said, "No harm done, I guess."

He didn't shake my hand.

I motioned to the bartender and said, "Give my new friend another beer on me. Hell, make it *two* beers."

At the notion of two free beers, Gentry's whole demeanor changed. He smiled, and said, "Well, thank you friend. That's mighty nice of you."

With that, I'd saved my ass from possibly getting skinned alive, and heard some very tall tales, too.

#

For the next several hours, I sat and listened to Gentry tell me some really tall tales; the time he hopped a train to Memphis, to see Elvis; the time he got in a fight with five Mexicans and whipped their asses; and the time he carried almost forty pounds of aluminum cans over his back for almost two miles to cash them in, among other tales.

I had to admit, for someone who was obviously full of shit, he had a way about him when it came to story telling, managed to be very convincing.

By mid-afternoon, three sheets in the wind and in fear I wouldn't be able to walk home without assistance, I had bid farewell to Gentry and the rest of the gang, and walked back home, with the sun at my back and feeling at least somewhat reinvigorated.

I was asleep on the couch by supper time.

THREE

For the first time in weeks, I slept like a baby.

I woke up around dawn the next day, and, after my usual shit shower and shave routine, I had sat down at my computer again, to see what I could come up with for my great American novel.

As is sat sipping single malt and staring at the screen again, it suddenly hit me that after all of these years, I had yet to finish my novel, or come up with an interesting subject to base it on.

But, never one to be easily defeated, I started typing away, basing my new story on my conversation with Dallas Gentry. If anyone could be considered an interesting subject to write about, it was him.

A few hours later, almost three sheets in the wind, and needing a break, I had adjourned to the front porch to take in some afternoon sunshine and relax my weary mind.

I hadn't been sititng there for long when the paperboy delivered the Wabash Valley Gazette. Upon glancing at the front page headlines, I couldn't believe what I was reading.

Dallas Gentry had been found by one of his neighbors, dead in his home, from a gunshot wound to the back of his head.

So much for relaxing my weary mind.

#

After composing myself, I'd gone back inside, sat down at the kitchen table, lit a cigarette, poured some more single malt, and continued reading the article on Gentry's untimely death.

To my horror, I read that he had shot and robbed for a grand total of less then forty-five dollars, some loose change, and some old yard sale grade jewelry.

I guess life really is cheap.

After reading the article, it had left no doubt as to what my next story would entail; a full length story about my day chatting with Gentry.

But, before I even had a chance to begin, there was a loud knocking at my door.

It was the police – wanting to talk to me about Dallas Gentry.

What a story this was going to be after all.

FOUR

The plain clothes cop who knocked on my door was named Harley Crow.

He was a tall, lanky fella with a big nose and beady little eyes. As we stood in my doorway exchanging social graces, I couldn't help but wonder why all Detectives, whether it be on TV or in real life, were always tall and lanky and had a big nose, but I kept that thought to myself.

As he stepped inside my apartment, I said, "Just take a seat at the table. Want some coffee? It's the instant stuff, but it's okay."

Sitting down, he smiled and said, "No thanks, I won't be here long."

I sat down too, sipped my single malt, and said, "So, Mr Crow. What can I help you with?"

Crow crossed his legs and said, "Mr Polanski, I understand that you spent a few hours yesterday afternoon, chatting with a fellow named Dallas Gentry."

I said, "Yes, I did. Very colorful character, he was, too."

Crow grinned and said, "Yes, he was. Very much so. What was it you fellas talked about all that time, if I may ask?"

I said, "Honestly? He did most of the talking. He had some really tall tales, too. I mostly just sat there and drank beer and listened to him."

Crow said, "Uh huh. So, he didn't do anything but feed you a lot of BS, and that's it? He didn't talk about money or anything else?"

I said, "Well, to be honest, he was flashing his money around, real proud he'd just cashed in some beer cans. I didn't think it was a very good idea, either, considering the crowd."

Crow said, "I have to agree with that," and was looking at me when he said it, like a scientist would study a lab rat. I didn't know whether to take it as an insult or not, so I just said, "Meaning?"

He said, "Meaning *nothing*, Mr Polanski. No offense intended."

I said, "No offense taken. But, I'm going to be very busy today. Is there anything else you want to speak to me about?"

Standing to his feet, Crow lit a cigarette and said, "No, that's all for now. I'm speaking with *all* of the patrons who were there yesterday. It's just a matter of police procedure, Mr Polanski."

Breathing a momentary sigh of relief, I said, "No problem, I understand."

Crow said, "Well, I better get going, I have other people to talk to today."

I walked him to the door, and as he walked out into the hallway, he said, "Mr Polanksi, don't stray too far away. I might need to speak with you again."

I said, "Where would I go?"

Then I shut the door in his face.

And sipped my single malt.

FIVE

By the time I had sipped about a pint's worth of my single malt, it was time for supper.

Having trouble deciding on either stale lunchmeat or TV dinners, I'd opted for a cold beer instead.

Then another.

I had to have some inspiration, you know, if I was to write about Mr Dallas Gentry.

And what better source of inspiration than the hair of the dog that bit me?

I was betting that Dallas would have felt the same about the situation.

So, I drink and I write.

#

By around ten pm, I had come up with about ten pages of the story – Gentry's story – and was pretty satisfied with it, so I decided to call it a night.

I walked out on the front porch, sat down in my ancient lawn chair, and sat gazing up at the full moon.

Except that night, it didn't look like a full moon. It looked like a big white skull, grinning at me, like it knew something I didn't know, something I *should* know, but was going to let the secret stay that way until I found it out for myself, the hard way.

Like always.

So, I sat and drank and stared at the moon and finally fell asleep in my lawn chair, and didn't wake up until almost dawn – and actually woke up hungry.

#

After a breakfast of instant oatmeal I'd found in the cupboard, I'd popped a cold beer and sat back down at my computer for another day of what I was hoping would be some productive writing.

As it turned out, my recent case of writer's block had all but disppeared, and I had a great day.

That is, until I read the newspaper again that afternoon.

Right on the front page was another article on the murder case, and it said that the police had several suspects, but hadn't made any arrests just yet.

The bad thing was, *my* name, well as several other bar partrons, was mentioned in the article as possible "witnesses" at the bar that day, seen chatting with Gentry.

It was then I knew what I had to do; I had to clear my own name – and find out *who* killed Dallas Gentry.

Talk about a great American novel.

9 798822 743043